SEEDS OF
L·I·G·H·T

Michael Dawson
Findhorn Foundation
June 90

PETER RENGEL

SEEDS OF L·I·G·H·T

INSPIRATIONS FROM MY HIGHER SELF

H J Kramer Inc
Tiburon, California

H J Kramer Inc
P.O. Box 1082
Tiburon, California 94920

Cover photograph by Michael Powers
Book and cover design by Abigail Johnston
Composition by Curt Chelin

Manufactured in the United States of America

10   9   8   7   6   5   4   3   2   1

MY PAL

This book is dedicated to Donna
Who continues to teach me Vulnerability
As we wander together through
Every nook and cranny of our Soul.

ACKNOWLEDGMENTS

A feeling of gratitude deep within my Heart goes out to:

Gale and Donna, for showing me that my Dreams
do come true!
Genny, for receiving this book with genuine appreciation.
Lynn, for providing the temple in which to write this book.
Sue, for being my sister and giving me helpful feedback.
Mom and Dad, for being available when I've really needed
them.
Matthew and Cyrus, for reawakening my love for children.
Ernie, for repeatedly trusting me throughout the years.
Hal, for following his Heart in deciding to publish this book.
Alex, for not telling me how hard it is to find a publisher.
Linda, for having so much fun editing this book with me.
Dan, for handling my ego delicately in the final phase.
The Wellesley House, for being full of such loving friends.
Diva, for showing me the present tense through a cat's eyes.

INTRODUCTION

A good way to absorb this experience is to first close your eyes and let your mind and body relax for a few minutes while gently placing this book over your Heart.

Then turn to the Table of Contents and run your finger down the titles to see which ones beckon you. Or just allow yourself to be guided to opening the book to the right page for receiving this moment's lesson, like drawing a Tarot card or throwing the I Ching.

When you read these selections, you may feel a deep stirring inside, caused by either your own strong positive or negative reaction. When one especially speaks to you either way, allow yourself to dwell upon it a bit. Read the selection called "Disowning." Then let yourself expand and allow whatever is stirring to become part of your own Being.

In any one sitting, just read a few that really touch you, even if you are tempted to go on. This allows some time for you to integrate and to become your own Truth.

Of course, this is all only my suggestion. As always, you have to find your own way to experience the best means of nurturing yourself.

TABLE OF CONTENTS

PROLOGUE

If you no longer need words
  To lead you to your Heart,
    Then close this book Now.

But if your mind needs assistance
  To stop judging and separating,
    Read on
      With all your Heart available.

1 · ACCEPTANCE

Acceptance is
Feeling Love in your Heart
For the highway patrolman
As he is writing you
A speeding ticket.

2 · ANGER

Your anger lets you know
You are judging and
Trying to control.

If you befriend your anger,
It will lead you
To accept "what is."

3 · ASKING

When you finally admit
You can't do it alone,
Asking the Universe
For some Help
Begins to set you Free.

In the very act of asking,
You begin to receive.

The next step is
To let go of all your Ideas
Of how the Help will come.

4 · BELIEVING

All spiritual belief systems
    Are attempts to reach
        The ultimate Truth.

When you go beyond belief,
    You discover
        Truth is
            A state of consciousness,
            Not an idea.

5 • BETRAYAL

It is impossible
  For someone else
    To betray you.

The illusion of betrayal can occur
  Only if you have expectations
    Of others being a certain way,
      And then they are different.

6 · BLISS QUOTA

What is your Bliss Quota?
  An hour per day?
    Or an hour per month?
      What are the limits of your Joy?

Find out how long you can feel
  Exquisitely contented.
      Consciously allow that time to increase.

Be aware of how uncomfortable it is
  To experience more Happiness than usual.

This awareness alone,
  Without doing anything else,
    Will allow more Love
      Into your Life.

7 · BLOSSOMING

Love is still a seedling
  When you experience it
    Alone.

Love blossoms
  When you share your Heart
  With another Soul.

8 · BOREDOM

Boredom is a quiet rage.

Allow your repressed anger to emerge
　And feel the deep urge
　　To move into Life
　　　Hidden within it.

You will not stay bored for long.

9 · CHANGE

Conscious change occurs by
   Shining the light
     Of awareness
      On unawareness.

Once you look deep inside and
   Clearly see your blindness,
     You need do nothing else.
      Change will unfold naturally.

10 · CHOICE

Your most profound choice
Each new moment in time
Is whether you are
In your head
Thinking
Or in your Heart
Being.

II · COMMITMENT

When you move deeply into Now with another,
  You feel a feeling
    Of being Committed
      As the walls of separateness
        Dissolve
          And you merge
            With the Other.

Commitment is a quality
  To be felt in the Present,
    Not a Promise for the Future.

12 · COMMUNICATION

Words spoken from the head
  Only perpetuate
    The mind/thought process.

Words spoken from the Heart
  Lead into a direct experience
    Of your own inner Silence
      From which your Truth emerges.

13 • COMPASSION

Compassion occurs
When you are feeling grief
For human suffering
While feeling the Beauty
Of human Love.

14 · COMPLETION

Life is an ongoing,
  An unfolding,
    With an infinite number
    Of loose ends.

The only thing
  You have to complete is
    Finally letting go of
      The idea of completion.

You are then free of the Past.

15 • CONCERN

The energy of concern looks humanitarian,
But is in fact a cancerous disease.

Concern judges by wanting others
To change in some way,
Usually by moving out of their pain
Because it hurts *you* too much.

The irony is
Your concern is
Actually impeding change.

By being stuck in your emotions,
You magnetize others into theirs.

When you are loving unconditionally,
You are making available
Your Heart's vibration
Which is the resolving energy
For Change.

16 · CONDITIONING

You are beginning to fathom
The depth of your Conditioning
When you experience that
Even beliefs as basic as:
"Your body must die"
Were lent to you
After you arrived
On this Planet.

17 • CREATIVITY

Your most creative act
  Is to embrace
    The Art of
      Simply Being.

Your ultimate creation
  Is your Life
    And how much Love
      You allow.

18 • D E A T H

Small ego deaths occur frequently,
   Followed by a rebirth
      Bringing forth a new you.

Learn to celebrate these mini-deaths,
   As they are only preparing you
      For the Death of your body.

If you are laughing with Death
   At the moment
      You leave your body,
         You will have no need
            To return
               To this Planet.

19 · DESIRE

Desire lies between
  You
    And
      Utter contentment.

When a desire arises out of
  The pool of absolute serenity,
    You have only a micro-instant
      To make a choice.

You can either stay relaxed in the pool
  And watch the desire rise above the surface
    Like a soap bubble
      Until it floats away...

Or you can grab onto the desire
  As it breaks through the surface
    And ride away with it
      Until your pool of serenity
        Is out of sight.

20 · DETACHMENT

Detachment comes through
  Knowing absolute attachment,
    Losing,
      And then feeling
        The excruciating anguish
          Of grieving your loss.
            Again and again.

Eventually,
  Feeling the anguish
    Leads to Joy in your Heart.

Now you are Free.

21 · DISCIPLINE

Discipline is
One of the most misunderstood
Spiritual concepts.

Discipline is *not*
Meditating at a certain time every day or
Exercising your body in the right way.

Discipline is
Being a spiritual warrior
By responding spontaneously
To your inner Truth
As it fluctuates
From moment to moment.

22 · DISCOVERING LOVE

Desire's
    Total absence
        Allows for
            Love's
                Total presence.

23 · D I S E A S E

Life on this Planet involves
   Embracing all change
      As the Universe presents it.

Disease occurs
   When you do not listen
      To the gentle tapping
         On the door of your limits.

If you ignore the gentle tapping,
   The Universe will knock
      Louder and louder
         Until eventually
            Disease renders you
            Defenseless.

Either old ideas must die
   So new ones can be born,
   Or your body must die
      So you can be reborn
         Into another chance.

24 · DISOWNING

A strong judgment or contraction
  Around particular persons or ideas
    Means only that you have yet
      To embrace their energy
        As your own.

The opposite is also true.
  When you meet a high vibrational being
    Or fall in love or enter a temple
      Or read inspirational writings,
        You often give your power
          Away to that person,
            Place, or idea.
This is disowning the positive within.

Strong contraction or soaring expansion
  Is the Universe's way
    Of knocking on your door
      Asking you to open and
        Look at your denial.
          Listen and include.

25 • EGO DEATHS

Pain comes from trying to resist
The daily ego deaths
Of parts of yourself.

Embrace Death
As a natural part
Of Life.

26 · EMBRACING

Everything that any human being
  Can possibly experience
    Is contained within you.

What is incredible is
  It is often easier
    To embrace
      The Devil inside
        Than the Christ.

27 · ENDING RELATIONSHIPS

The emotional intertwinings
  Which bind you
    As you fall into Love's illusions
      Become the knots of imprisonment
      When you are trying to get free.

      As the knots come undone,
        What awaits is a combination
        Of grief and relief.

          If you become lost in the grief,
          You miss the relief.
          If you allow for both,
          You end with
            A new beginning.

28 · ENLIGHTENMENT

Enlightenment
  Is like
    Death.

      Both are already
        On their way
          To you.

          So relax...
            And have a good time,
              Until one
                Or the other
                Or both
                  Arrive.

29 · EXPANSION

The Universe gently taps upon the outer edges
  Of all you have embraced
    Of this earth plane's Reality.

If you hear the tap
  And open to include
    More,
      You will feel
        The exuberance of expansion.

If you ignore the tapping,
  It becomes a knocking,
    Then a pounding,
      Demanding to be included.

The pounding becomes
  More and more painful
    As the Universe cracks open
      The brittle boundaries of your ego.

By listening
  For the gentle tap of the new,
    You can save yourself
      A lot of useless suffering.

30 • EXTERNAL REALITY

External reality
  Can be either
    Thick
      Or thin.

Thick
  When you make it so real
    That you lose your Self into it.

Thin
  When you stay within your Self
    And just enjoy the drama,
      Be it comedy or tragedy,
        Romance or mystery.

The thinner the external,
  The more Joyful the internal.

31 • FEELING

When you label your emotions
As either good or bad,
You build a wall of judgment
Between yourself
And your experience.

Just feeling the juice of Life
Within the energy of all emotions
Creates self-acceptance.

32 · FLOATING

Float
  Float
    Float your boat
      Gently down the stream.

Merrily
  Merrily
    Merrily
      Merrily
        Life is but a dream.

Since it is all just a dream,
  Why make the effort to row?
  Why not just float
    With the flow?

33 • FLOWERING

A flower appears
  When a green plant enjoys
  A prolonged orgasm.

34 • FORGIVENESS

Feeling forgiveness
  Is a beautiful release
    From the prison of the past.

But in order to forgive someone,
  You first have to have judged them
    As wrong.

Let go of judgment
  And you will never need
    To forgive again.

Sounds great, eh? But don't worry,
  You will need to forgive again,
    Because you will judge again,
      Because you are human.

Don't let high-sounding Spiritual Ideals
  Destroy your acceptance
    Of who you are
      Right now.

35 • FREEDOM

Orgasm is freedom from Time.
Death is freedom from Time and Space.
Love is Freedom.

36 · FRIENDSHIP

A Friend
  Is someone
    Who moves you
      Into
        Your Heart's vibration.

A Friend
  Is someone
    Who sees your Love,
      Even when
        You don't.

37 · THE GAME OF LIFE

You have boundaries around
  How deeply you have accepted
    The totality of this Reality.

You are constantly presented with situations
  Just beyond your present capacity
    To embrace.

You either
  Reject the lessons
    And remain stuck
      In the pain of the status quo
        Or let go
          And feel the Joy of expanding.

These are the rules of the Game.
  The choice is yours.

38 · GIVING

True giving occurs when
After having given,
You have More
Instead of Less.

39 · G O D

God is a vibration
　Continually showering
　　Love.

God is an empty void
　Available to receive all
　　You choose to give—
　　　Be it Love or Hate,
　　　　Bliss or Anger.

As you become vulnerable and receptive,
　You attune to Love,
　　And your vibration harmonizes
　　　With the Song of God.

40 · GRACE

You can try to manipulate
   The Universe into giving you
      What you want,
         Or you can open
            To receive Grace
               Without expectation.

With Manipulation,
   There will be an effort,
      No matter how subtle,
         As you *try* to receive.

With Grace,
   You will be totally surprised
      By a gift more precious
         Than any of your Dreams.

41 · GRATITUDE

Gratitude is a feeling
  Experienced in your Heart,
    Not a thought form
      Inside your head.

Feeling Gratitude
  Brings with it
    Feeling more Gratitude
      For the Blessing of
        Feeling Gratitude.

42 • THE GREATEST GIFT

The greatest gift
        You can give
                Is to truly receive
                        Another Human Being.

43 • G R E E D

Greed is
  A desire for more
    Combined with
      A feeling of unworthiness.

This combination
  Causes you
    To grab
      Instead of
        Allow.

44 • GRIEF

Contained within
  Your tears of grief
   Is all the Love
    You have for your Friend
     But did not fully express
      When you were together.

45 · GUILT

Guilt is self-anger
  For repressing
    Rather than expressing
    Your deepest Truth.

46 · HEALING

Healing has nothing to do with
  A Healer
    Doing something
      To someone.

Healing has to do with
  Human Beings
    Being,
      Melting together
        Into the Present Tense.

Then a miracle occurs.
  Everyone receives Love.
    All are emptied of Darkness
    And filled with Light.

The depth of this Transformation
  Depends on Trust,
    Vulnerability,
      Receptivity,
        And a willingness
          To allow Change.

47 · A HEALTHY DIET

What you eat cannot create
   Higher states of consciousness
   Or even good health.

When you stay out of the way,
   Food is naturally transformed
   Into pure energy.

48 · IMPRISONMENT

Feeling your longing
  For something more to Life
    Lets you know
      You are imprisoned.

Following the voice
  Of your longing
    Leads you to risk Change
      Which unlocks the doors
        To Freedom.

49 · INFINITY

Dive into an atom.
 You will find
  The Whole of Existence.

50 · INNER PEACE

Inner Peace has nothing to do with
    Feeling calm inside.

Inner Peace is
    Allowing your experience
        Each moment in time.

In one moment,
    Inner Peace may mean
        Weeping tears of sorrow.
In another,
    Allowing your anger.
In yet another,
    Feeling rapture
        At seeing the Beauty
            Of newborn Life.

Each moment brings Inner Peace
    If you don't judge yourself.
        Celebrate all
            Your human qualities.

51 • JEALOUSY

The gift of Jealousy is that
Its involuntary explosion
Can set you free
From illusions you have
About being in control
Of your emotions.

Welcome to the Human Race.

52 · JUDGMENT

Judgment is
　To Love
　　What
　　　Cancer is
　　　　To the body.

With one big difference—

When Judgment arrives,
　Love instantly dies.

53 · LAUGHTER

The lightness of Laughter
And the light of Love
Walk hand-in-hand
Down the Path of
Happiness.

54 · LISTENING

The ears of your mind
   Either
      Listen to sounds
        Or
          Listen to thoughts.

Try directing your Awareness
   Into experiencing sound
      As pure energy.

As your Awareness flows
   Down the river of sound,
      Your thoughts become still
      And you are Here, Now.

55 · LOST AND FOUND

To think
  You have found
    The Answer
      Is to be Lost.

        To Embrace
          The Mystery of Life
            Not knowing
              Is to be Found.

56 · LOVE

57 · LOVERS' ILLUSION

When you are in Love,
  You rest deeply in the Present.
    Forever
      Occurs within
        Each timeless moment
          Together.

When you return to linear Time,
  The mind wants to reconstruct
    Forever
      Into a promise for the Future.

But Forever never exists in the Future.
  It is only contained
    Within the deepest recesses
      Of the Present.

To chase Tomorrow's Promise
  Is to miss
    The True Forever
      Within Now.

58 · LOVING YOURSELF

Loving yourself is
    Accepting yourself
        Even when
            You are not
                Accepting yourself.

59 · L U S T

Lust can disguise itself
　As Love
　　Only when you have failed
　　　To become Lust's friend.

Enjoy the burst of Life from within,
　But do not be fooled
　　Into Love.

Lust knows no Heart,
　But the Heart
　　Can include Lust.

60 · MEDITATION

Real Meditation has no techniques
  Because your mind would only
    Become attached to them.

There are no guided fantasies
  Because they only perpetuate imagination.
There are no solutions
  Because there are no problems.
There are no answers
  Because they make questions seem real.

There is only you
  Here
    In this moment
      With an opportunity to open your Heart
        And find inner Silence
          Where Love and Nurturance
          Await you.

61 • MEETING

When strongly attracted to someone
And excited to greet them,
You get pulled out of your body
As you go out and
Try to meet them.

When your energy is
Outside of yourself
Looking to connect,
No one is left at Home
For them to meet.

True meeting takes place
Within the sphere
Of your own
Inner Light.

62 · MONEY

The day you let go of the idea that
   Money is compensation for working,
      Your whole orientation toward
         Living on this earth plane
            Will dramatically shift.

Receiving money can be
   The natural result of
      Following your Heart
         And doing exactly
            What makes you Happy.

By opening to this possibility,
   You are well on your way to
      Transforming your relationship
         To money,
            To work,
               And to play.

63 • MY FRIEND THE FLY

One of my greatest Teachers
  Was a fly who befriended me.

As he sat on my hand contentedly
  Rubbing his head with his front legs,
    I fell in love with his miracle.

And I felt his Love in return.

When he stopped rubbing his head,
  I felt disappointed and
    Wanted him to do it again.

As my desire entered,
  He flew away
    Because he felt my lack of
      Unconditional acceptance.

I instantly recognized what I had done,
  And asked him for his Forgiveness.

He flew back gently onto my hand
  And began to rub his head again.

This time I appreciated him
  Even after he stopped,
    And our Love continues
      Within my Heart
        Even to this day.

64 · NO/YES

Sometimes
   Saying Yes to someone else
      Obscures your own Truth.

Sometimes
   Saying No to someone else
      Affirms your own Truth.

What is important is not Yes or No,
   But to go with whichever brings
      Peace to your Heart.

65 · N O W H E R E

Did you ever stop to realize
  Nowhere is both
    No where
      And
        Now here?

Where is it
  You are headed
    In such a hurry?

66 • ON THE SAME SIDE

When you and your Lover disagree,
The important thing is
You both feel you are
On the same side,
Facing the issue.

Stay beside each other,
Looking out at the conflict
Together,
Rather than putting it
Between you.

This feeling of togetherness is
Much more precious
Than any problem
You will ever solve.

67 • ORGASM

You usually create an Orgasm
   By using energy from a thought form.
      With an appropriate image,
         An Orgasm is triggered.

But a deeper kind of Orgasm awaits
   When a thought-free energy
      Begins pulsating
         Through your whole Being.

As this pure energy takes over,
   You are swept into
      Another Reality
         Where Time is not
            And Perfect Silence is.

All Desire is born out of
A feeling of incompleteness.

Discovering that absolutely
Nothing outside of yourself
Can fulfill you
Is both Devastating
And Exquisite.

Devastating
Because you lose
Your desire for
Worldly Achievement.

Exquisite
Because you find
A new Freedom
To fly
Inward.

69 • P A T I E N C E

Perhaps you came to this Planet
    From a Reality where
        Thought manifests
            Instantly into form.

It may be difficult for you
    To get used to the time lag
        Between internal change and
            External manifestation.

With this understanding,
    You can experience internal change
        And then knowingly Trust
            That it will appear
                In your external Reality
                In its own good time.

70 · P O W E R

If you change your concept of Power
From exerting your Will
To get what you want
Into surrendering your Will
To the flow of Life,
You transform Reality
From Doing to Being.

71 · PROBLEMS

You can never find the resolution to a Problem
   Within the same Level of Consciousness
      Where it was created.

If you shift into a Higher Vibration,
   The Problem will not even exist there.

But do not worry. It still awaits you
   In the Vibration where you created it
      If you want to go back and visit.

Now you may ask, and wisely so,
   "How do I shift into other
      Levels of Consciousness?"

The methods vary from Person to Person
   And from Moment to Moment.

Perhaps by looking inside with Awareness.
   Or meditating to open your Heart.
     Or feeling the Problem's Pain.
      Or feeling Nature's Beauty.
       Or moving into Sexuality.
        Or receiving a Hug.
         Or dancing.
         Or singing.

Whatever way you choose can work
   Only if you allow yourself
      To become Vulnerable enough
       To move out of your head
        And into your Heart
         To receive Love.

72 · PROMISES

The only Promise
You can ever make
Is to never make
A Promise.

73 · PROTECTION

Your most effective weapon
Is to allow yourself to be
Totally Vulnerable
To the sword
Of your enemy.

If and only if
You become Defenseless
Will you see your enemy
Drop his sword
And
Become your Friend.

74 · RECEIVING

The Universe will support you
    Financially, Emotionally,
        Sexually, and Spiritually
            Far beyond your Dreams.

Receiving
    Requires the Courage
        To follow
            Where your Heart leads
                Instead of
                    Being Victimized
                        By your Fear.

75 · RELATING

Relating is real
  Because it unfolds
    In the Moment
      Between two Free
        Individuals.

Relationship is an illusion
  Created by the Mind
    To promise security.

When Relating
  Becomes Relationship,
    A structure is created
      Which dissolves Now
        Into Hopes and Dreams
          And Expectations.

76 · RESIGNATION

Resignation is fear of taking a Risk.
  It surpasses cancer and car accidents
    As the number-one cause of Death...
      Except...

With this kind of Death,
  Instead of your body decomposing,
    Your Life itself disintegrates.

So be courageous enough
  To feel the Fear
    And
      To take the Risk.

If you fail,
  So what.
    I you succeed,
      So what.

Within the energy of Risking
  You find
    The essence of Life.

77 · SADNESS

The Beauty of Sadness
  Lies in its Depth.

The Heights of Ecstasy
  You are able to experience
    Depend upon
      The Depths of Despair
      You have touched.

So when a wave of Sadness arrives,
  Allow yourself to ride on it.
    Let it wash over you.

Lose yourself into Sadness
  And you will find a new Self
    On the other side of the Tears.

78 · SAMENESS

The outer mind creates labels
　　Like "Jewish" or "Christian" or "Hindu,"
　　　　Making our Paths appear to be different.

But we're all travelling up the same mountain.
　　We each have the same Inner Realizations
　　　　As we discover Love's Unfolding.

If we stop listening to these labels
　　And start listening to our Hearts,
　　　　Then we can join as One
　　　　　　In celebrating our Humanness.

79 · SATORI

The deepest Bliss I have ever known
   Came when my Desires were completely gone.

My Being was available to do anything,
   From vacuuming floors to cutting string.

Others' Will to get things done
   Became my own, as we were One.

This state lasted for several weeks,
   Then came to a halt with a sudden Screech.

All had been Yes, without a hint of No,
   But then came back that powerful Ego.

"I" returned with all its might.
   Again there was "me" to put up a fight.

In just one moment it all changed from Bliss
   Into an exploration of the deepest Abyss.

But now I have tasted Pure Love a lot,
   And I know, "Truth is, when I am not."

80 · THE SEED OF SILENCE

To use techniques to Change
　Your Belief System
　　Is missing the point.

　　　You are substituting
　　　　One thought form for another,
　　　　　But still remain stuck
　　　　　　At the level of the Mind.

Dive in deeper to find
　That tiny Seed of Silence
　　Buried beneath the surface
　　　Of all Thoughts.

　　　Very tenderly and gently
　　　　Water that delicate seed
　　　　　With Love
　　　　　　So it can sprout.

As it grows, your Mind's hold
　Becomes weaker and weaker
　　Until you are Free.

81 • THE SEEKER

Desiring a new car
  Is no different from
    Desiring Enlightenment.
     Both take you away
      From this moment.

And yet,

If your desire for a new car is fulfilled,
  It will be replaced by
    An endless stream
     of new desires.

If your desire for Enlightenment is fulfilled,
  You will be replaced
    By an endless stream.

82 • SEXUAL ENERGY

Real Sexual Energy bursts forth
  With only a Feeling of pure Lust
  And a need to express it.

The Vulnerability necessary
  To share this pure Lust is
    Often too frightening
    For you to allow.

Sharing the depths of your Fear
  Creates an Intimacy
    From which
      Genuine Sexual Union
      Can emerge.

83 · S E X U A L   L O V E

Sex is renewed
    By risking All,
        Every Time.

84 · SILENCE

The most direct way
 To communicate your Truth
  Is to speak
   The Language of Silence
    With a fellow Human Being.

85 · SNEEZING

A Sneeze
  Is just
    Your nose
     Having
      An Orgasm.

So be total and enjoy.

86 · SPIRITUAL EGO

Once it is clear that
  Your primary purpose on the Planet
    Is to evolve Spiritually,
      The next step is
        To find Freedom
          From the Desire
            For Spiritual
              Achievement.

87 · THE SPIRITUAL PATH

When you are enjoying the walk
    And can't even remember
        You are on a Spiritual Path,
        Then you are
            Totally Blessed.

88 • SUFFERING

Suffering is the coating of avoidance
   You use when you are afraid
      To experience emotional pain.

If you allow yourself
   To feel the pain,
      The pressure of repression
         Is released like a valve.

Both pain and suffering dissolve into Joy.

89 · SUICIDE

Embrace your Suicidal Self
  Until you feel it might well be
    The only sane part of you.

Only then are you
  Truly Free
    To choose Life.

90 · SUPPORTING YOURSELF

Have you ever noticed
How much easier it is
To give your support
To someone else
Than to yourself?

You can use the same voice
Which knows your friend can do it
To let yourself know
You can do it too.

91 · SURRENDER

Total Surrender involves
Witnessing your Ego
Participate in the World
With no Investment
Or Judgment.

92 · TOGETHER

Touching Souls
  In Silent Union,
    Mind becomes Empty
      Heart becomes Full.

93 · TRANSFORMATION

As the Light enters
And dissolves the Darkness,
Be gentle with yourself
As you see yourself
Clinging to the Old
And fearing the New.

Even when the New is
Exactly what you want,
You may still feel
Unworthy to receive
Your Heart's Desire.

Give yourself Time
Instead of Guilt.
Allow yourself
A few mistakes.
After all,
You are only Human.

94 • T R U S T I N G

Trusting means
  Letting go
    Of Control.

Trusting means
  Allowing
    Others to move
      In any Direction.

Trusting means
  Dropping
    Your cherished Beliefs.

Trusting means
  Sensing
    When to surrender
      To the Mystery
        Beyond yourself.

95 • TRUSTING YOURSELF

Trusting Yourself means
  Allowing *Whatever* is
    Bubbling up Inside
      To overflow
        Without Judgment.

Trusting Yourself means
  Listening to your "negative" Voices
    With an ear attuned to learning
      Whatever they have to teach you.

Trusting Yourself means
  Enjoying all of You,
    In all your Humanness.

96 · T R U T H

Truth is
A Vibration
To attune to
Energetically.

97 · TUMESCENCE

Tumescence occurs when you have
  An overabundance of energy
    And nowhere to channel it.

Tumescence expresses itself
  In the form of Bitchiness,
    Either blatant or covert.

If you and your Lover find yourselves
  Quarreling for no apparent reason,
    Stop for a moment,
      Smile knowingly,
        And shout, "Tumescence!"

Then allow Lust to flow
  Through you freely
    Until you are both
      Back in your bodies,
        Glowing with Smiles
          Of Contentment.

98 • UNDERSTANDING

Truth lives
  Where Understanding
    Is Not.

      Let go of your Desire
        To Understand
          For it imprisons you
            At the Level of Thought.

          Dive Deeper into
            Trust and Awe!

99 · VULNERABILITY

Vulnerability is the Key
  Which opens the Gateway
    Between Thinking and Feeling.

Once you leave the Realm of Thought
  And enter the Sphere of Feeling,
    The Domain of the Heart
      Is only a Breath away.

100 · W H Y ?

Any Answer to
"Why?"
Is always
A Lie.

It is *not*
In your mind
That the Truth
You will find.

AFTERWORD

There were no Entities
  Channeled through me
    As I wrote this Book.

There were no Gurus involved,
  Nor did I tap into any Secret
    Ancient Mystical Teachings.

The Source of this Book is
  My Life Experience,
    My Humanness, and
      My observations of
        This Incredible Mystery!

My greatest Support comes from
  Continuing to Learn
    How to Allow and to Trust
      Love's Love and Grace
        To Carry my Life.

E P I L O G U E

One of the hardest parts of creating this Book is to freeze
it in Time by printing it in one final form. Many times
when I go back and read a page, I want to rewrite it
because my Truth keeps changing.

So just understand that these views only represent one
moment in Time, and will inevitably change for both you
and me as we dive deeper into our Selves.

An interesting part of having these words remain con-
stant is to see that on different days the same words can
say something entirely different to me.

Aren't we Humans so very fascinating?

Who is creating this Miracle anyway?

*Peter Rengel is currently conducting parenting classes;
meditation evenings; chakra/energy classes; and love, sex,
and relationship groups. If you would like to contact him,
write Peter Rengel, P.O. Box 77, Mill Valley, CA 94942.*

Books That Transform Lives

BOOK I THE EARTH LIFE SERIES
LIVING WITH JOY
by Sanaya Roman, Channel for Orin
*"I like this book because it describes the way I feel
about so many things."*—VIRGINIA SATIR

BOOK II THE EARTH LIFE SERIES
PERSONAL POWER THROUGH AWARENESS
by Sanaya Roman, Channel for Orin
"Every sentence contains a pearl..."—LILIAS FOLAN

OPENING TO CHANNEL:
HOW TO CONNECT WITH YOUR GUIDE
by Sanaya Roman and Duane Packer, Ph.D.
*This breakthrough book is the first step-by-step
guide to the art of channeling!*

WAY OF THE PEACEFUL WARRIOR
by Dan Millman
*"It may even change the lives of many...
who peruse its pages."*—DR. STANLEY KRIPPNER

TALKING WITH NATURE
by Michael J. Roads
*"From Australia comes a major new writer...
a magnificent book!"*—RICHARD BACH

H J Kramer Inc
AMERICA'S FASTEST GROWING NEW AGE SPIRITUAL PUBLISHER